Money Math

A Math Practice Workbook for Kindergarten through Grade 3

Pages from this workbook may be copied for educational purposes.

Certain images within this workbook were used with permission from FrontDesk studio.

Table of Contents

Introducing the penny

Practice writing the word penny!

penny penny penny

A penny is worth 1 cent. Did you know that when you see this symbol ¢ it also means cent?

This is President Abraham Lincoln, 16th president of the USA

This is what a penny looks like. It is small and brown. You've probably seen one before.

Front

Back

Color in the amount:

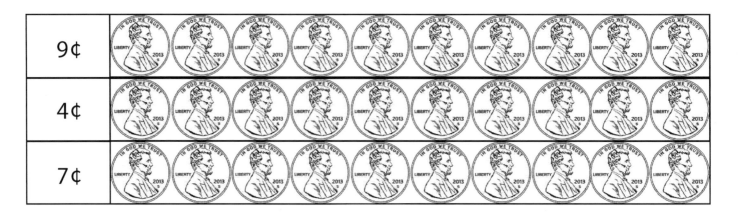

9¢	
4¢	
7¢	

Color in the amount:

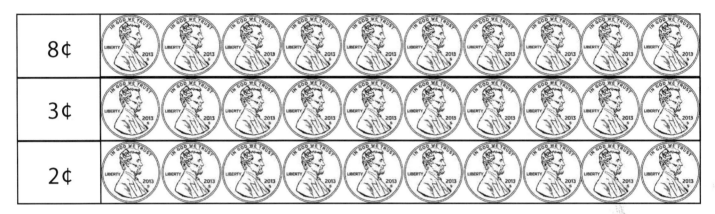

8¢	
3¢	
2¢	

Draw a line to match the picture with the correct amount.

5¢

3¢

4¢

Anthony wants to buy a piece of candy for 5¢. Color in how many pennies he needs.

Sarah needs 3¢ to buy a gift for her friend. Color in how many pennies she needs.

Now Sarah needs 8¢ to pay for gift wrap for her present. Color in how many pennies she needs.

How much money is in my piggy bank?

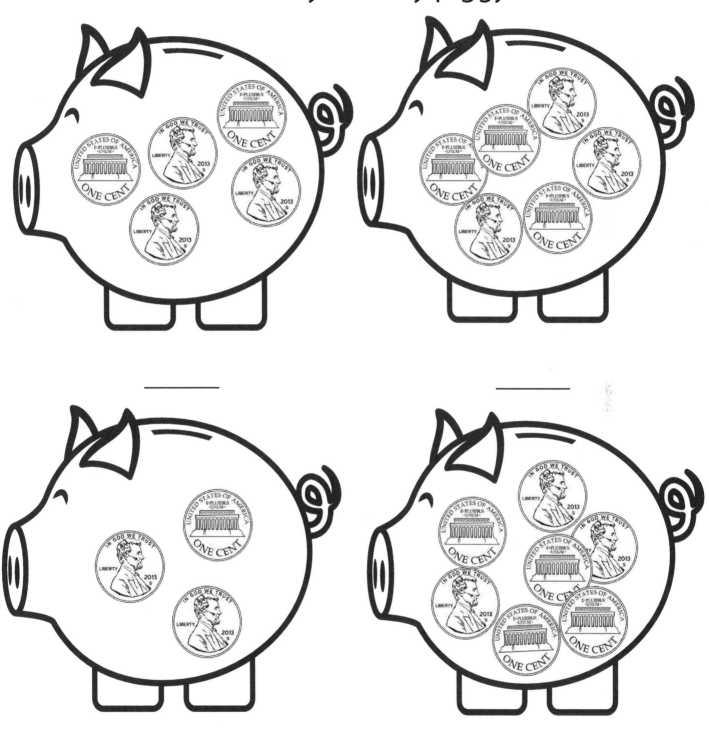

_____   _____

_____   _____

How much money is in my piggy bank?

_____   _____

_____   _____

Introducing the nickel

Practice writing the word nickel!

nickel nickel nickel

A nickel is worth 5 cents.

This is what a nickel looks like. It is small and silver, and slightly bigger than a penny.

This is Thomas Jefferson, 3rd president of the USA

Front   Back

Let's practice counting by 5! Fill in the blanks.

_5_ _10_ ___ _20_ _25_ ___ ___ _40_ ___ _50_

___ ___ _70_ ___ _85_ ___ _100_

Skip counting by 5

Fill in the blanks:

5 ___ ___ 15 ___ ___ ___ ___

___ ___ 10 ___ ___

___ ___ ___ ___ 20 ___

___ ___ ___ ___ ___ 25 ___

Can you skip count by yourself from 5 to 100? Fill in the blanks:

_5_ ___ ___ ___ ___ ___ ___ ___ ___ ___

___ ___ ___ ___ ___ ___ ___ ___ ___ _100_

Draw a line to match the picture with the correct number

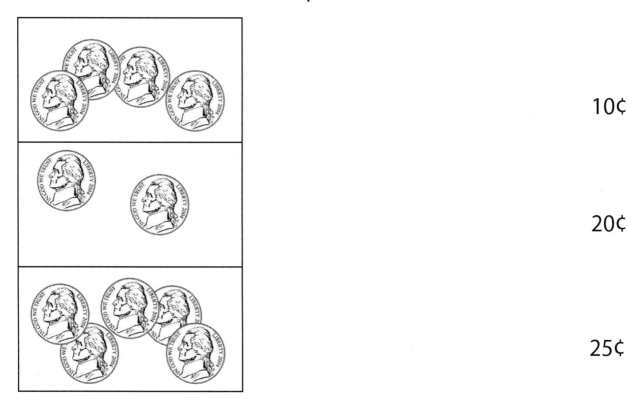

10¢

20¢

25¢

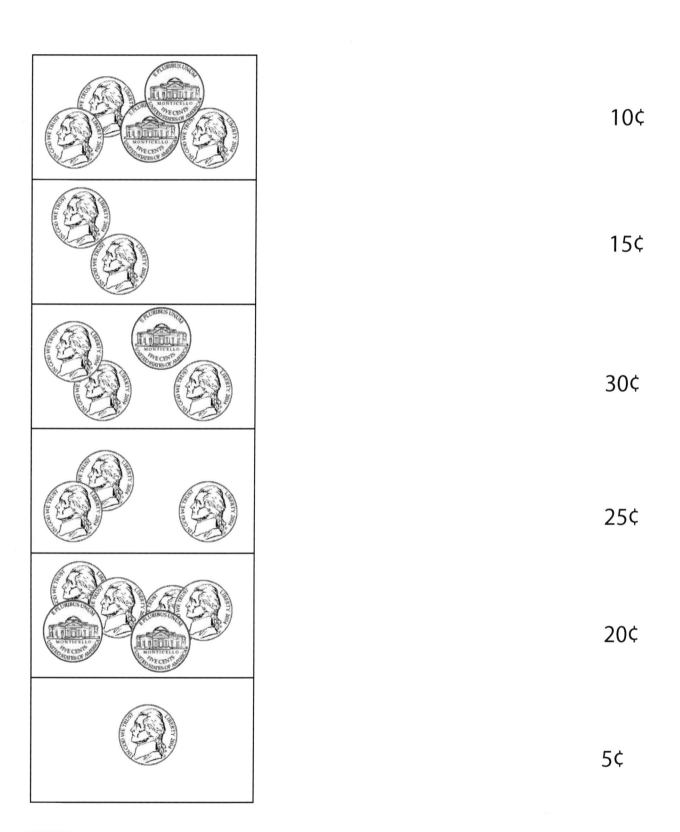

10¢

15¢

30¢

25¢

20¢

5¢

Counting pennies and nickels

Count the pennies and nickels and write in the total amount.

penny = _____ ¢

nickel = _____ ¢

Example:

= ___7___ ¢

= _____ ¢

= _____ ¢

 = _____ ¢

 = _____ ¢

 = _____ ¢

 = _____ ¢

= _____ ¢

 = _____ ¢

= _____ ¢

 = _____ ¢

 = _____ ¢

= _____ ¢

Shopping with nickels

Circle or color in how many nickels you need to buy the item.

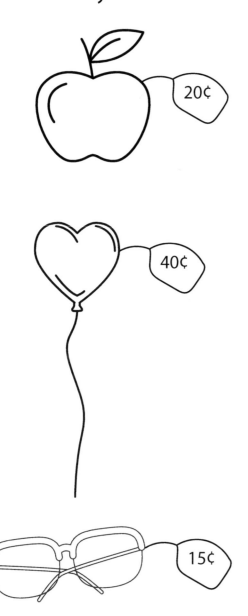

Shopping with nickels

Margo has 3 nickels in her pocket.

She wants to buy this pencil for 10¢. Does she have enough money? Check yes or no.

_____ yes

_____ no

Margo goes back to the store. This time she has 5 nickels in her pocket.

She wants to buy 2 pencils. Does she have enough money?

 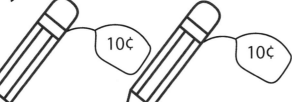

_____ yes

_____ no

Shopping with nickels

Circle or color in how many nickels you need to buy the item.

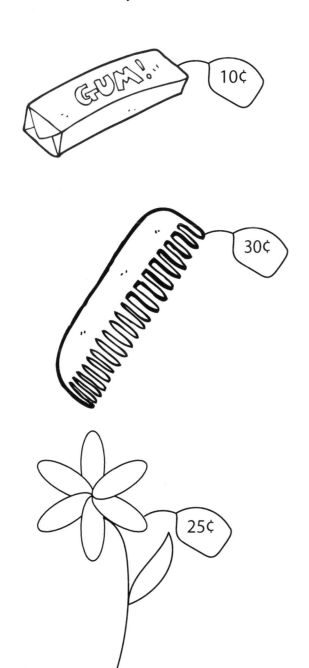

Shopping with nickels

Circle or color in how many nickels you need to buy the item.

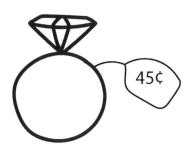

Introducing the dime

Practice writing the word dime!

dime   dime   dime

A dime is worth 10 cents.

This is what a dime looks like. It is small and silver, even smaller than a penny.

This is Franklin Delano Roosevelt, 32nd president of the USA

Front   Back

Let's practice counting by 10! Fill in the blanks.

10 ___ 30 ___ ___ ___ 70 ___ ___ 100

Skip counting by 10

Fill in the blanks:

10   20   ___   40   ___   ___

___   ___   30   ___   50   ___   70

10   ___   ___

___   20   ___   ___   ___

Can you skip count by yourself from 10 to 100? Fill in the blanks:

10   100

How much money do I have in my piggy bank?

_____ ¢

_____ ¢

= _____ ¢

= _____ ¢

= _____ ¢

= _____ ¢

= _____ ¢

Shopping with dimes

Circle or color in how many dimes you need to buy the item.

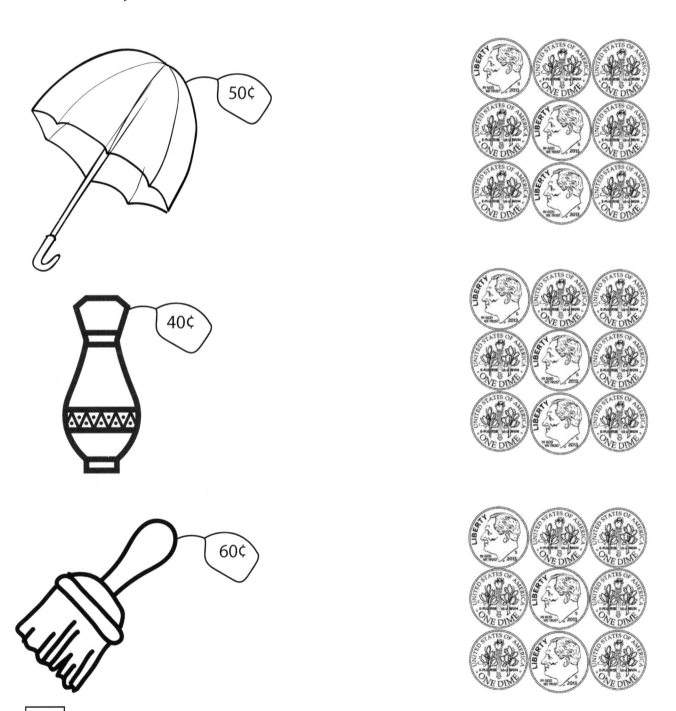

Shopping with dimes

Circle or color in how many dimes you need to buy the item.

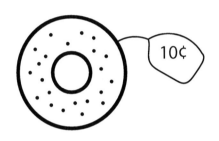

Shopping with dimes

Olivia has 4 dimes in her pocket.

She wants to buy this shirt for 90¢. Does she have enough money? Check yes or no.

_____ yes

_____ no

Olivia goes back to the store. This time she has 2 dimes in her pocket.

She wants to buy this plant for 75¢. Does she have enough money? Check yes or no.

_____ yes

_____ no

Introducing the quarter

Practice writing the word quarter!

quarter   quarter

A quarter is worth 25 cents.

This is what a quarter looks like. It is silver, and bigger than a penny, nickel and dime!

This is George Washington, the 1st president of the USA

Front   Back

Do you know how to count by 25?

25   50   75   100

Skip counting by 25

Fill in the blanks:

25   ___

___   50   ___

___

___   ___   75   ___

Can you skip count by yourself from 25 to 100? Fill in the blanks:

<u>25</u> ____ ____ ____

Color in the correct amount:

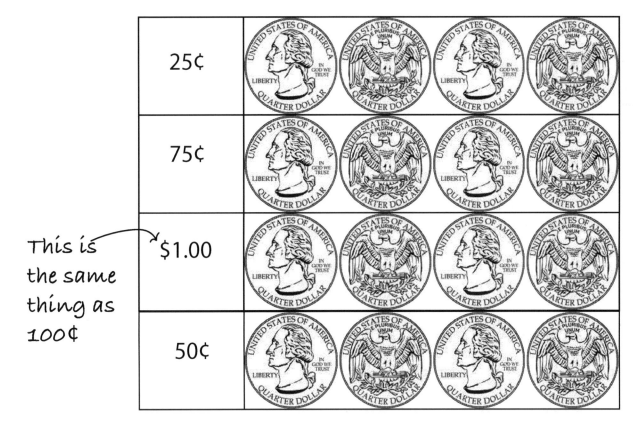

This is
the same
thing as
100¢

 = _____ ¢

 = _____ ¢

 = _____ ¢

 = _____ ¢

= _____ ¢

 = _____ ¢

 = _____ ¢

 = _____ ¢

 = _____ ¢

 = _____ ¢

Shopping with quarters

Circle or color in how many quarters you need to buy the item.

Shopping with quarters

Circle or color in how many quarters you need to buy the item.

Shopping with quarters

Asher has 3 quarters in his pocket.

He wants to buy this boba tea for 80¢. Does he have enough money? Check yes or no.

_____ yes

_____ no

Asher goes to another store. This time he has 2 quarters in his pocket.

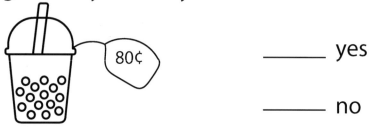

This store is selling boba tea for only 50¢. Does Asher have enough money to buy it this time?

_____ yes

_____ no

Identifying Coins

Write the name of the coin in the space next to it.

Example:

Nickel

_____

_____

_____

_____

_____

_____

_____

_____

Identifying Coins

Find and circle all the pennies on this page. Can you find all 8?

Identifying Coins

Find and circle all the nickels on this page. Can you find all 8?

Identifying Coins

Find and circle all the dimes on this page. Can you find all 8?

Identifying Coins

Find and circle all the quarters on this page. Can you find all 8?

Counting pennies, dimes, nickels and quarters

Count the coins and write in the total amount.

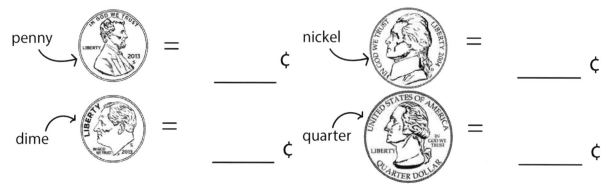

penny = _____ ¢   nickel = _____ ¢

dime = _____ ¢   quarter = _____ ¢

Example:

= _____36_____ ¢

= _____ ¢

= _____ ¢

Counting Coins

= _____ ¢

= _____ ¢

= _____ ¢

= _____ ¢

= _____ ¢

 = _____ ¢

 = _____ ¢

 = _____ ¢

 = _____ ¢

= _____ ¢

 = _____ ¢

 = _____ ¢

 = _____ ¢

 = _____ ¢

 = _____ ¢

= _____ ¢

= _____ ¢

= _____ ¢

= _____ ¢

= _____ ¢

 = _____ ¢

 = _____ ¢

 = _____ ¢

 = _____ ¢

 = _____ ¢

Look inside Isabel's piggy bank. Circle or color in how much money she should take out to buy the item.

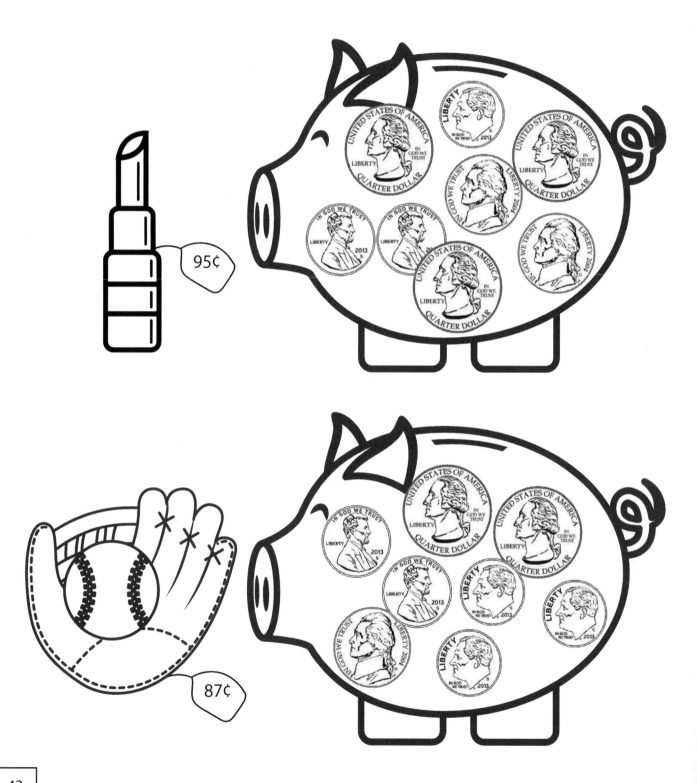

95¢

87¢

Look inside Isabel's piggy bank. Circle or color in how much money she should take out to buy the item.

86¢

47¢

Look inside Isabel's piggy bank. Circle or color in how much money she should take out to buy the item.

Look inside Isabel's piggy bank. Circle or color in how much money she should take out to buy the item.

75¢

26¢

Look inside Isabel's piggy bank. Circle or color in how much money she should take out to buy the item.

Making exact amounts of money

Look at the price tag for each item. How many dimes, nickels, and quarters will you use to pay? Try to use as few coins as possible.

Example:

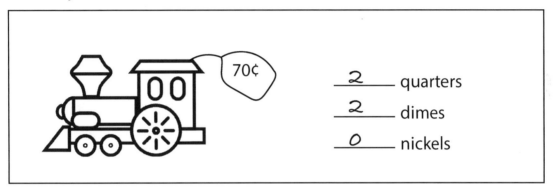

70¢

_2_ quarters
_2_ dimes
_0_ nickels

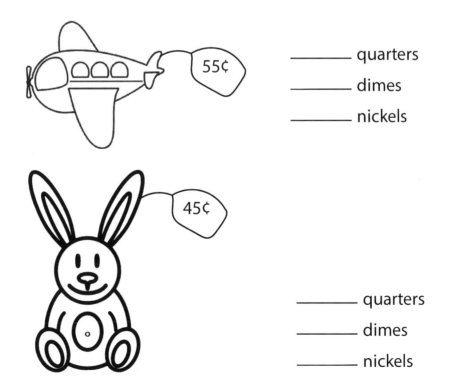

55¢

_____ quarters
_____ dimes
_____ nickels

45¢

_____ quarters
_____ dimes
_____ nickels

15¢

———— quarters

———— dimes

———— nickels

95¢

———— quarters

———— dimes

———— nickels

30¢

———— quarters

———— dimes

———— nickels

85¢

———— quarters

———— dimes

———— nickels

Counting Coins

_____ quarters

_____ dimes

_____ nickels

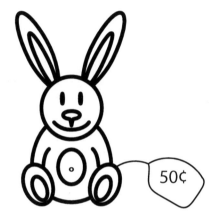

_____ quarters

_____ dimes

_____ nickels

_____ quarters

_____ dimes

_____ nickels

_____ quarters

_____ dimes

_____ nickels

50

—————— quarters

—————— dimes

—————— nickels

—————— quarters

—————— dimes

—————— nickels

—————— quarters

—————— dimes

—————— nickels

—————— quarters

—————— dimes

—————— nickels

Amanda used 4 coins to buy this bouncy ball for 80¢. What coins do you think she used?

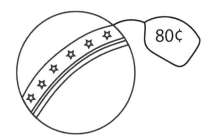

_____ quarters

_____ dimes

_____ nickels

Brandon used 3 coins to buy these blocks for 60¢. What coins do you think he used?

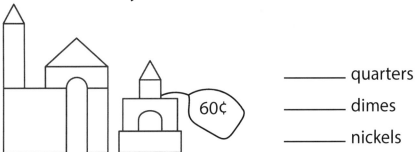

_____ quarters

_____ dimes

_____ nickels

Avery used 5 coins to buy this basketball for 25¢. What coins do you think she used?

_____ quarters

_____ dimes

_____ nickels

Austin used 3 coins to buy this ice cream cone for 35¢. What coins do you think he used?

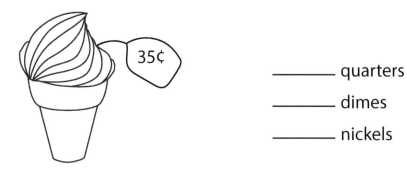

_____ quarters

_____ dimes

_____ nickels

Austin used 3 coins to buy this lollipop for 75¢. What coins do you think he used?

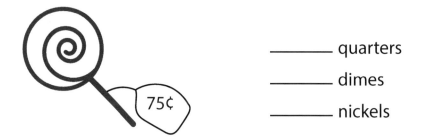

_____ quarters

_____ dimes

_____ nickels

Austin needs to brush his teeth after all that sugar! He used 8 coins to buy this toothbrush for 80¢. What coins do you think he used?

_____ quarters

_____ dimes

_____ nickels

Introducing the dollar bill

Practice writing the word dollar!

dollar dollar dollar

This is what a one dollar bill looks like.

Front

A dollar is worth 100 cents!

Back

This is George Washington!

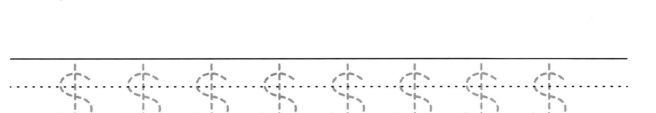

This symbol is called a dollar sign. Practice writing it here:

$ $ $ $ $ $ $ $

Different dollar amounts

The dollar bill comes in 6 differents
amounts: 1, 5, 10, 20, 50, and 100!

One dollar four different ways

Count the coins and fill in the blanks:

1 dollar = _____ pennies

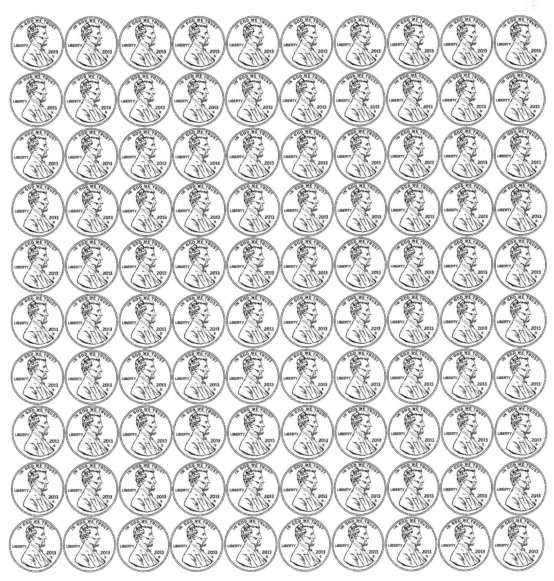

1 dollar = _____ nickels

1 dollar = _____ dimes

1 dollar = _____ quarters

Counting with dollar bills

Practice adding up the dollar bills. Write in the total.

Example:

$ __65.00__

$ _____

$ _____

$ _____

$ _____

$ _____

$ _____

$ _____

$ _____

$ _____

$ _____

$ _____

$ _____

$ _____

$ _____

Counting Dollars and Cents

Practice adding up the dollar bills and coins. Write in the total:

$ _____

$ _____

$ _____

$ _____

$ _____

$ _____

$ _____

$ _____

$ _____

$ _____

$ _____

$ _____

$ _____

$ _____

$ _____

Shopping with Dollars and Coins

Draw a line to match the picture with the amount of money needed to buy it.

$2.40

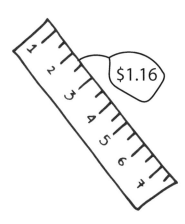
$1.16

$6.02

Shopping with Dollars and Coins

Draw a line to match the picture with the amount of money needed to buy it.

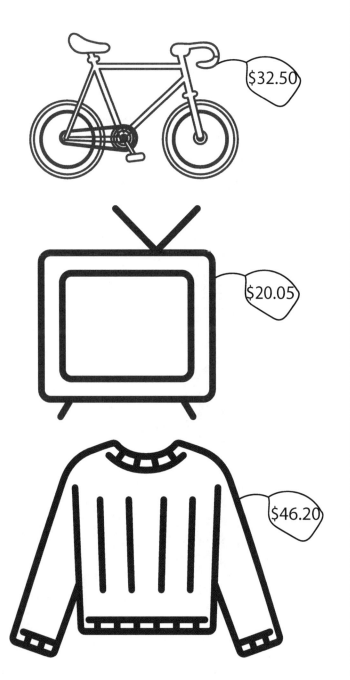

$32.50

$20.05

$46.20

Shopping with Dollars and Coins

Draw a line to match the picture with the amount of money needed to buy it.

Shopping with Dollars and Coins

Draw a line to match the picture with the amount of money needed to buy it.

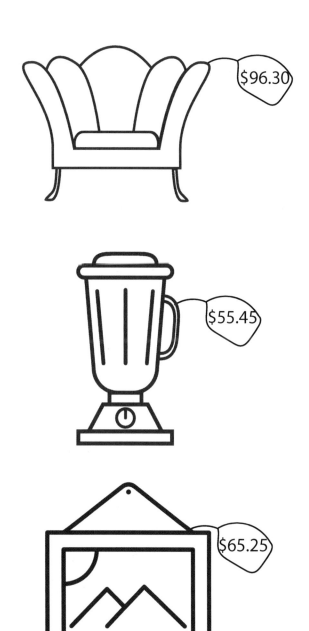

Making Change with Coins

Calvin wants to buy something for 85¢. Color in what coins he should use to buy it. Write in what his change will be.

¢ _____

Aiden wants to buy something for 37¢. Color in what coins he should use to buy it. Write in what his change will be.

¢ _____

Sophia wants to buy this box of tissues. She has 3 quarters what will her change be?

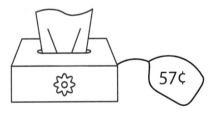

57¢

¢ _____

Making Change with Coins

Lucy buys a cookie for 38¢ and pays for it
with 2 quarters. What is her change?

¢ _____

McKenna gives the cashier 2 quarters and
3 dimes. She gets 5¢ back in change. How
much did the item cost?

¢ _____

Roman wants to buy this rose.
He has eight dimes. How much
will his change be?

75¢

¢ _____

Making Change with Coins

Henry buys a bottled water for 27¢ and pays for it with 3 dimes. What is his change?

¢ _____

Theo gives the cashier 1 quarter and 3 nickels. He gets 4¢ back in change. How much did the item cost?

¢ _____

Nevaeh wants to buy this pear. She has 3 dimes and 1 nickel. How much will her change be?

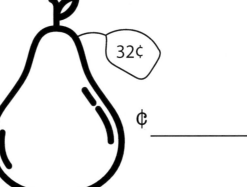

32¢

¢ _____

Making Change with Coins

Ryan is buying an apple that costs 65¢ with 3 quarters. How much will his change be?

¢ _____

McKenna gives the cashier 3 nickels. She gets 4¢ back in change. How much did the item cost?

¢ _____

Carla wants to buy this dress. She has two quarters. How much will her change be?

¢ _____

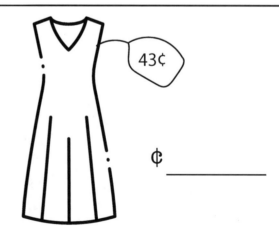

Making Change with Coins

Louis wants to buy something for 55¢. Color in what coins he should use to buy it. Write in what his change will be.

¢ _____

Danny wants to buy something for 63¢. Color in what coins he should use to buy it. Write in what his change will be.

¢ _____

Tanya wants to buy a box of chocolates for 35¢. She has 2 quarters what will her change be?

¢ _____

Making Change with Dollars

Jack wants to buy this pizza for $6.00. He pays with a 10 dollar bill. What will his change be?

$6.00

_____

Peter wants to buy this pillow for $3.00. He pays with a 5 dollar bill. What will his change be?

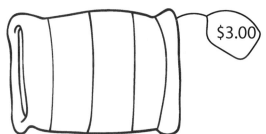

$3.00

_____

Alex wants to buy this clock. She has 20 dollars. What will her change be?

$17.00

_____

Making Change with Dollars

Tommy wants to buy this notebook for $12.00. He pays with a 20 dollar bill. What will his change be?

 $12.00

_____

Peter wants to buy this backpack for $7.00. He pays with a 10 dollar bill. What will his change be?

 $7.00

_____

Liz wants to buy this calculator.
She has a 50 dollar bill. What
will her change be?

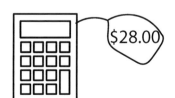 $28.00

_____

Making Change with Dollars and Coins

Blanche buys something for $6.67. Color in what bills she should use to make her purchase. Write in what her change will be.

_____

Mel wants to buy something for $12.94. She has a ten dollar bill and a 5 dollar bill. What will her change be?

_____

Luke wants to buy this mirror. He pays with a 20 dollar bill and a 5 dollar bill. What will his change be?

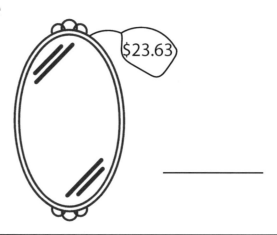

$23.63

_____

Making Change with Dollars and Coins

Ruby buys something for $1.56. She pays with two dollar bills. What will her change be?

_____

Lola wants to buy something for $10.37. She has a ten dollar bill and 2 quarters. What will her change be?

_____

Lindsey wants to buy this bottle of shampoo. She pays with a 20 dollar bill and a 5 dollar bill. What will her change be?

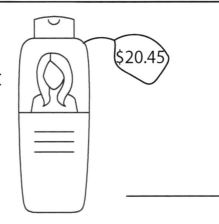

$20.45

_____

Making exact amounts of change

You are the cashier at a shop! Look at the price tag and the amount of money the customer offers. Then write in how many dollars, quarters, dimes, nickels, or pennies you will offer as change.

Example:

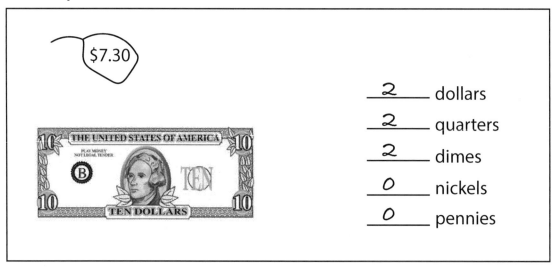

$7.30

  2   dollars

  2   quarters

  2   dimes

  0   nickels

  0   pennies

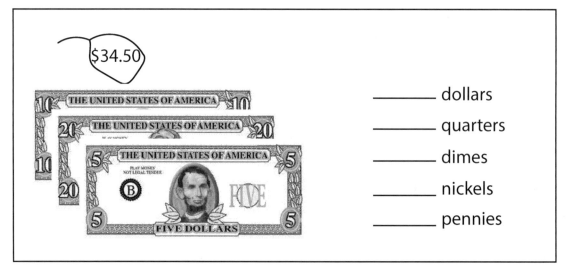

$34.50

_____ dollars

_____ quarters

_____ dimes

_____ nickels

_____ pennies

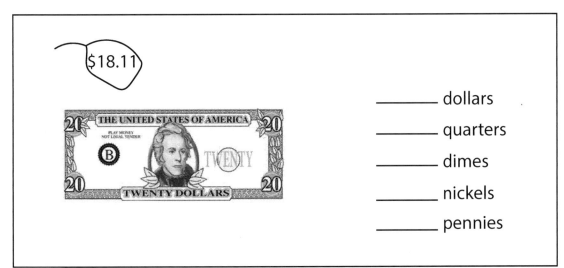

$18.11

_____ dollars

_____ quarters

_____ dimes

_____ nickels

_____ pennies

$1.71

_____ dollars

_____ quarters

_____ dimes

_____ nickels

_____ pennies

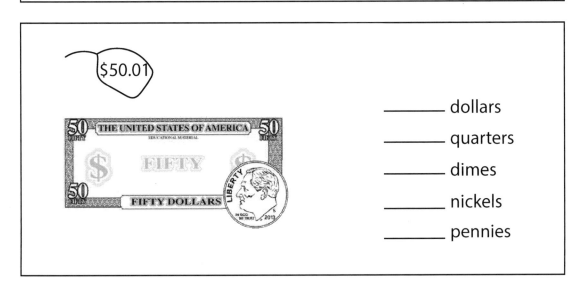

$50.01

_____ dollars

_____ quarters

_____ dimes

_____ nickels

_____ pennies

_____ dollars

_____ quarters

_____ dimes

_____ nickels

_____ pennies

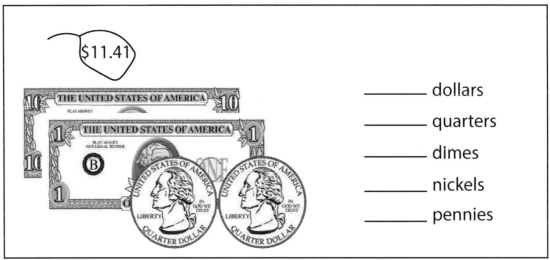

_____ dollars

_____ quarters

_____ dimes

_____ nickels

_____ pennies

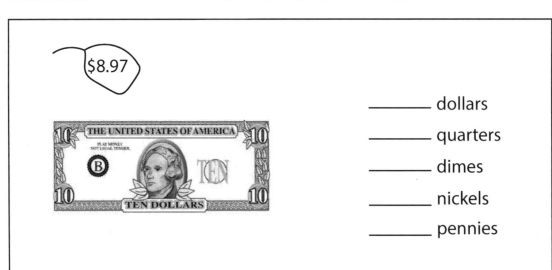

_____ dollars

_____ quarters

_____ dimes

_____ nickels

_____ pennies

_____ dollars

_____ quarters

_____ dimes

_____ nickels

_____ pennies

_____ dollars

_____ quarters

_____ dimes

_____ nickels

_____ pennies

_____ dollars

_____ quarters

_____ dimes

_____ nickels

_____ pennies

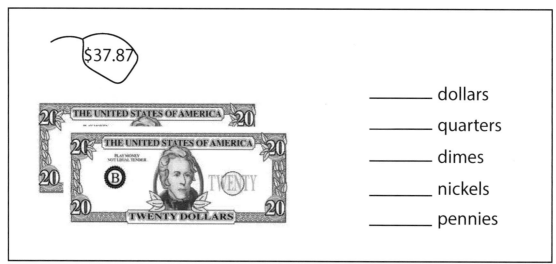

_____ dollars

_____ quarters

_____ dimes

_____ nickels

_____ pennies

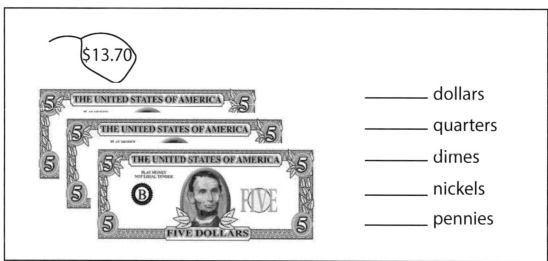

_____ dollars

_____ quarters

_____ dimes

_____ nickels

_____ pennies

_____ dollars

_____ quarters

_____ dimes

_____ nickels

_____ pennies

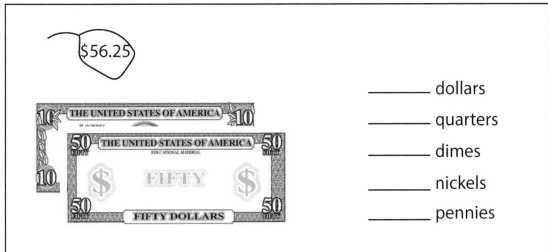

$56.25

_____ dollars

_____ quarters

_____ dimes

_____ nickels

_____ pennies

$3.70

_____ dollars

_____ quarters

_____ dimes

_____ nickels

_____ pennies

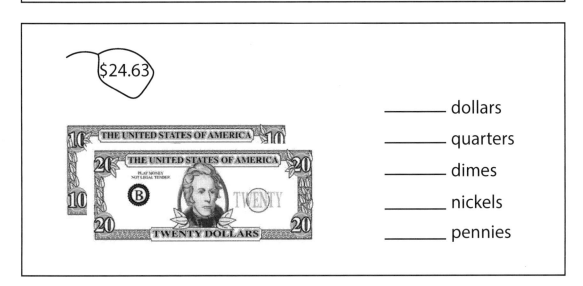

$24.63

_____ dollars

_____ quarters

_____ dimes

_____ nickels

_____ pennies

Made in the USA
Columbia, SC
27 February 2023

13064647R00048